Let Me Speak!

By

Becky Chadburn

Contents

A prologue

Hi there!!

My name is Becky I am sharing this journal,

With others to share my story,

I've had ups and downs,

I will make you laugh, cry and everything in between,

This is my story and this is in my words,

I am a survivor of domestic violence and mental health,

This book has enabled me to understand,

My emotions, feelings and thoughts,

I hope many people will read this,

I hope it will help many people,

This is my journey and this is my poetry journal.

Absorbed

I absorbed everything that tried to break me apart,

You tried to break my heart,

I stayed focused and didn’t give into your temptations,

I gave myself redemption, I stayed content,

One thing you can never take from me is my perseverance,

You can never take away my resilience,

I was born to prosper not hide,

No matter what you did I didn’t give in,

I didn’t give up,

Don't stand to close,

I've been down this road before,

Don't look, don’t touch,

You can't handle me I’m too much,

Don't fall to fast,

Your taunting fogged up the glass,

I'll break the ice,

Don't blame me for not being nice,

You rolled the fucking dice,

No more miss nice,

I'm just here to pick up my remaining pieces,

Don't stand to close,

No more second chances,

I am breaking out of my cages,

Am I too hot to handle,

I breathe the air into my lungs,

I take the world to its knees,

You tried to break me,

I will burn this fucker down,

You’re chained up and hell bound,

You will never see me around,

I absorbed you and suffocated you, you fucking prick.

All time low

I'm at an all-time low, now I let my emotions flow,
Letting my heart find its glow, you'll reap what you sow,
I'm trying to find a way to let it go, I don't care if I'm alive or dead,
AHH! I need to get these things out my head, how loud do I have to shout,
I need to block this out, I carry on, and on this path I've faced many a challenge,
Fuck! I need to make a change, my feelings are so significant, I need to shine,
Ever so bright, I'll give it one hell of a fight and take flight,
Shit! I hope I'll be alright, I have been broken,
I'm letting it all out now I have spoken,
I'm still at an all-time low, But I'm no longer alone,
My darling your ready it's time now for you to go home.

Alone

I'm standing alone on the ropes, I needed fixing the most,
I'm a soul that's lost, Welcome to my fire,
I'm climbing up my spire,
All my life I've been packed with prescriptions,
I've got big ambitions, I'm facing my dark days,
These voices are getting louder in my head,
I'm not my own friend, all my life I just pretend,
Shit! Another bad decision,
You fucked up the pieces of my brain,
I try and smile without lying,
My happiness are you buying?
You don't know my life,
I'm not vague, I'm a heartbreaker,
This isn't yet over, I'm hiding my pain,
Let's live life fast, Fuck all of my past,
I'm my own critique, I'm going to live and learn,
Can you hear me? Or am I imaginary,
You don't know me I'm extraordinary,
Didn't you hear what I said?
I'm reinventing myself,

Testing me are you daft?

Fuck you, you prat,

I'm a bad mother fucker,

Oh shit! Here I go again.

Bank

They go to you as a revolving bank, like money can fill up a tank,
You're coming up empty and sank, always there when you need money,
Isn't it funny, The bank of Sharon,
Who do you think I am do you think I'm a baron,
Always there when you need cash, then bang! Their gone in a flash,
Always others making us clash, Best friends till the end,
I'll always be your friend, always others getting in our way,
Always others ruining our day, all the others we fuck of and dash,
I love it when it's just me and you, why can't it just be us two,
Facing the world together, Sharon and Becky
We go together like peanut butter and jelly,
Why do people creep in our dome?
Why can't they just leave us alone?

Becky Stay Awake

I can see your teary eyes, I don't know where my mind goes,
You can tell me all you need to say, are you moving away,
Will you let me stay? I can hear you screaming,
I can hear your heart beating, Stay awake,
Becky stay awake, it's okay, Memories stacked into boxes,
Gain back your control, I'll catch you when you fall,
Becky stay awake, I'll help you, I'll help you find yourself,
I can hear you screaming, I know you're on the edge of breaking,
Becky stay awake, Rise up, I know you're tired,
I'll be all you required, Fight it'll be alright,
Fight with me tonight, Give it your all,
Becky don't give up, Becky don't stop,
Becky keep going, Becky stay awake.

Best Friend

My best friend, Isn’t funny to have a friend to tell everything too,
You're always there when I need you,
I love our long conversations,
She's my safe station,
Simply sitting on our phones for hours while we go about our day,
Even when we have nothing to say,
I won't let you down, you make me happy when I frown,
You're my angel with a crown,
She's the light to my darkness,
She's always there even in all my weirdness,
Always there to light my way,
I tell her all my little secrets with no judgment,
She's the one who's there threw every event,
She's the post who keeps me on the straight,
With her by my side, I'll be alright,
Together we fight, we take on the weights of the world together,
I'll leave her side never,

They call her Sharon rock,

She will always be the key to my padlock,

She will always be my best friend and my love for her will never end.

Better Days

I'm not who I was before, I'm stronger,

I'm better now, I'll be brave

I won't be afraid, People will tell my story,

I was this girl who never backed down,

I was the girl who always won,

I am better now, I took moments to be myself,

I'll light up the sky with lightening,

If I'm to go down I'll go down fighting,

I'm not afraid of the thunder,

Your the one who will be going under,

I was born to wander,

You don't know me I'm a monster,

I'm a grenade, I'm a renegade,

You the one that will need a bandage,

My secrets give me an advantage,

I won't stop, I won't give up,

I'm better now, I'll leave you to rot here in the mud,

Testing me won't do you any good,

I'm bringing it back to me,

I'm better now, The rain isn't permanent,

I'm dancing in the sun, I'm so proud I made out of the storm,
Better days are coming, Better days are coming,
I've been a soldier, I know I've been fighting for years,
It's my time to shine, I'll be fine,
I'm on the other side of the storm now,
I don't know how I made it,
I'm still standing fighting for it,
I got threw all the shit,
I found the will and the strength to get threw it,
The rain isn't permanent, Even the skies cry,
When life gets to heavy,
You can look at me with envy,
You don't know my bravery,
I'm climbing up this ivy,
I'll do what I do best, I'll pass your test,
I'll leave you terrified, You're either beside me or in my fucking way,
You better move,
This battle against me you will lose,
So much better now, I'm better now
Better days are coming,
I'm better now

BPD

It’s the fear of abandonment, I'm just looking for something more,
All I can feel is emptiness, I don't know who I am,
This shadow follows me around, Am I just mad that my brain is tapped,
I'm trapped in the way that I act,
But you’re refusing to leave me till my brain has been taken,
Maybe I’m just mistaken, do you feel like breaking down,
Shit it's making me down, I feel out of place, like I just don't belong anywhere,
Does anyone even need me around, nobody understands me,
You just want to see me break down,
Damn! Here you are again,
Can you just fuck off with the pain?
All they can offer me is therapy,
Talking therapy they say is that the only way,
I'm drowning within my mind, Feeling like I’m never enough, I'm doing my best,

Can you please just give me some rest, I'm shattered on the floor and I'm bleeding,
How do I get rid of this feeling, I'll stick around, I'm not leaving,
I'll keep it all on the inside, Can I just run and hide, Fuck it!
I'll just leave it behind, I'm silent when I cry,
Everyone just throws they're issues on top of mine,
Don't fret I'll worry about both at the same time,
I just don't belong anywhere,
Is anybody listening, I'm ashamed of it, I can't quit,
The mistake was always mine for thinking that anybody cares,
Fuck! I've been trapped in your snare,
I'm embracing all my fears, relighting all my fires,
Don't try and tell me what to do with the hurt that you gave me,
Borderline personality disorder is what they label it,
Like you can just put a label on this shit!
What that's just it, saying my brain is fucked, what,

I can't control my anger, I look in the mirror,
All I can see is a stranger, I can't let me down again,
If feeling isolated, maybe my hearts out dated,
I'm breathing for the last time, it's impossible to breathe,
Bpd its being at war with yourself, don't quite get a moment,
I sustain myself on the idea that I will be okay eventually,
How can I love anyone when I don't know who I am?
Unresolved fear, anger and distress from childhood,
Maybe I'm just no good, I can't cope mentally,
I'm giving up eventually, nothing seems real,
Drinking just to feel, I question if I really do exist,
My thoughts I resist, No impulse control, I won't let it define me,
I look to god and say please, I've been running since I was a child,
As an adult I'm afraid to look behind, I'm a sinking ship that's burning,
Please hold hand, don't let go of my hand, Save

me as I hit the ground,

Because I needed you around, But Bpd she said.

Broken

I feel numb, I'm an empty shell of a person that you all made me into,
I have no sense of identity, I look to others and share my empathy,
I'm not empty, I have so much love to give, and myself I forgive, Stuck alone in the rut,
All the times I said yes but, all the loss I face, I've lost my place,
I've lost faith, every path has been a mistake, I carry on, on the basis I can face this,
You hate my presence I can feel the pressure building up inside of me, I'm a prisoner of my own brain,
When will I escape this strain, I keep my heart under caution, So many words stuck in my head,
I often wonder if I'd be better off dead, I keep on moving with a smile and my ever shining light,
I'll be the be brightest star in this darkening night,
People try to poison my mind,
Myself is who I find, I keep on moving, I carry on,
Maybe I'm better off alone or maybe I'm just

made of solid stone,
I am a flame you can't contain, I'm breaking free from my restraint, my heart you won't stain,
You see my vulnerability and prey but me you underestimate, I look at you and say hah check mate,
You saw my light and tried to put me out, I pick up my broken pieces and shine even brighter,
I hold myself even tighter, I am a fighter and I will not be broken.

Built up

I guess it all built up to this, who do you think you are,

Do you think you're a super star, I ran so fucking far,

I will never say never, to make it right I will fight,

Whenever you knock me down I will not stay on the ground,

I myself will pick up, I will face you in court,

Me you won't hurt, Locked up now and they won't let you out,

I won this last fight, I will use my last breath to say all I need to say,

I will have my closure and after that you can be eaten by a vulture,

I'm not afraid of you, I'll have my last say,

I'll hammer that last nail in your grave,

C'mon Becky be brave, now he's bigger than me,

Stronger than me, He hasn't battled the wars I have,

I'll fight you in combat, You're a twat,

None the less I will beat you, I was born from fire,

I’ve been raised in the ashes, I'll bring my full force,

If push comes to shove, I'm made from ice water and blood,

After court you can just rot here in the mud,

I conquered the giant, now I’ve got the world in my hand,

You won't leave me pinned to the ground, the moon is where I will land,

You I will confront, I'm not going to say this bluntly,

Don't think you got one over on me today,

I'll have the final say, then I’ll be on my way.

Bullet proof

I will dream until I make it real,

I will chase the sun, my life has now begun,

I am dreaming it possible,

Every bullet you shot at me I dodged,

I'm chasing every star,

I'm running near and far,

I'm relentless, I must confess,

I am not a quitter, I will never quit,

My dreams are coming alive,

I am writing my own book and having it published,

I will accomplish all my dreams,

When I greet the devil, I will grin at the evil,

Evil is my middle name,

I will make Satan hang his in shame,

I've already played this game,

I had already given up many times before,

I won't lie, I won't die,

Do you wanna hold my heart or do you wanna try to pull me apart?

I knew they would be people like you,

Trying to pull me in two, Should I be terrified,

Hah! Don't make me laugh,

I will leave you gassed,

I am a fucking pyscho, you don't know me,

You don't wanna,

Na na na I want to start a fight,

You don't know me I'm a sinner,

I'll make you wanna do a runner,

I am a winner, every bullet you shot at me I dodged,

I cannot be shot.

Call

You can call me weak stop calling,

You can call me crazy,

You don't know my bravery,

You can call me a slut,

Is that because I'm too hot,

A slut it something I'm not,

I won't let you control my life,

This is my fuck you and goodbye,

You can call me fragile,

But I'm full of life,

You can call me a narcissist,

You I dismiss,

You can call me an inbred,

Is that because I'm not in your bed,

You can call me a psycho,

Stop calling,

You can tell me how to dress,

You won't make me a mess,

You're no different from the rest,

You can tell me how to do my hair,

Don’t be so unfair,

You won’t put out my fire,

You can tell me who to talk too,

I'll see right threw you,

You can try and control me,

I'll be free,

I am me,

You can call me what you like,

But stop fucking calling.

Can’t

I can't find words to write, for myself I will always fight,

Undrawn curtains, My life isn’t certain, No motivation to do anything,

Just sitting there while days slip away, I have nothing left to say,

My mind feels clouded, I feel like a child being grounded,

Same shit different day, Days spent in the same clothes,

Un brushed hair life’s so un fair, Conversations I’m not really having,

I'm there but I’m not really there, Like my body is there but my mind is elsewhere,

I feel stuck not knowing what to do or where to go,

I feel like I’ve grounded to a halt, I look back at my life,

I ask myself was it my fault,

Living in a jolt, Pain shooting threw me like a lightning bolt,

Days spent wasting away, endlessly scrolling threw the social media page,

Looking at shit people post, Shit! I feel so lost,

This life of mine does cost, I can feel the frost,

My reaction doesn’t even give me satisfaction,

Am I just writing just as a distraction?

My feelings have got me distraught, For myself I have always fought,

All I wanted was a bit of support, it’s getting dark in this heart of mine,

Am I at the end of the line, When will I be fine, When will I be alright,

Even my own family don't give a shit about me, all about whose doing the best,

While I’m out here facing my biggest test, facing it all alone,

Oh well! I guess I will face it on my own,

The reality to others my life to them is unknown,

Nobody knows the suffering in me, I'm a bitch yeah I agree,

I just want to go and find a quiet place by the sea,

Where I can be me.

Cant back down

I've got my feet on the ground, I know where my heart is,
Writing a poem doesn't make me an artist, I'm just trying to get somewhere,
Trying my hardest, I won't be the person everyone else wants me to be,
You either love me or hate me, Fuck it you didn't have to date me,
I'll just keep on moving, myself I won't be losing,
I've been told I'm not good enough a million times, I try to be positive,
How can I be so negative, I'll be okay in time, my hand start to shake'
Did I make a mistake, maybe I'm just being paranoid,
All my life I've been a little mad bastard, every weekend on a mad one plastered,
I know they put me threw a lot of shit, I'll get threw it, Maybe I am just a bitch,
All I ever wanted was an apology, Let down yet again by the authority,

I guess I’m just a minority, I won't apologize for being this way,
All those bastards made me this way, I know my emotions are drastic,
I'll bounce back like fucking elastic, so don’t you be so sarcastic,
I don't care what have to say, knock yourself out,
Cus yet again I will fight, I'll always find my way, in myself I can commit,
You couldn't even write this shit, I'm in a fucking nightmare,
Come on fight fair, seriously I don't want to be near ya,
I’ve been left behind, myself I can find, I am more than you'll ever know,
I'll stay and smile for a while, I'll just fake fine, I get it right next time,
Fake it till you make it as the saying goes, I'll embrace all their blows,
I’ve got my head above water, You I will slaughter, You won't stop me,
I’ve gotta keep going, I don't wanna be a little psycho but I might be though,
I'm shattered standing right there, So don't you

fucking tell me that you care,
No one ever walked in my shoes, your so boring you make me wanna snooze,
Fuck it! I'll just drink the booze, I'm a beautiful nightmare,
Falling into the pits of despair, Am I just past repair?
It's getting cold out here, I won't run away from it now,
I'll get threw it somehow, I'm fighting the strongest the battles,
I'm in the strongest storm, Fuck it I'm on form,
For you I won't perform, I'm going to stand here and fight for it,
I'll stand here and fight with you, I'm reaching for the clouds,
I won't back down, you won't see me drown, like dory says keep on swimming,
Cus in this battle I am winning, I'll leave you with your head spinning,
I'll just laugh and walk away grinning, you have me around, you won't see me hit the ground,
I'm starting to feel nervous, Welcome to the circus, when the guns go of I won't take cover,

I'll just go and sit by a river, I know I'm a pain in the arse,
But let's be together right here right now,
I want to go to a place where it's just you and me,
I'm in serious mess and I feel seriously lost
I'm standing alone in a crowded room, Will you tell me everything is okay,
So many things I wanna say I keep silent all because I don't want to upset people with the truth,
So instead I kill myself slowly, I'm losing myself just a little,
Why couldn't they have met me in the middle, I'll take my heart and I'll burry it right here in the sand,
I'm gravitating above the ground, I'll get a box and lock away my tears,
It's been this way for years, you can break my bones but you won't see me fall,
I'm not walking alone, I'll stop me from falling down,
How did I get into this mess, when people try to put me down I'll just smile and walk away,
I only have to answer to myself, I'm breaking the

silence,

Spreading awareness for domestic violence,

Thank you for sharing this story with me,

You couldn’t even write this shit,

Welcome to my life.

Careless helpless little man

From you I still run

Why couldn’t you do the right thing

Why pain is all you bring

I hope I can find away

You could have walked today

Saw you trying to still win

Ah where to begin

I looked at you on a screen

I didn't fucking feel a thing

I smiled under my mask

My hearts beating fast

You want to play your stupid games

I'll fucking show you my flames

You do not know what I am fucking capable of I sat there with my head held high

I let out a giggle of a sigh

I saw the fear in your face

As I sat there and put you back in your fucking place

I saw you nearly cry

Knew I was there couldn't see me ahaha

I'll take this all the fucking way
I will suffocate you
Your innocent you pretest
Give it rest
You will not fucking break me
You don't stand a fucking chance
See the difference is I'm not a fucking coward like
you
I will stand my ground
I will see you next time mother fucker
I keep warning you I'm a monster
I have the fucking strength of my mother and
nan,
I fucking can
I deserve better than this
Why do you need to take the piss
You will feel the full force of my fist
For you my blood thirsts
Careless helpless man
I'm the light in the darkness
I will not fucking bow down
Not now nor ever
I stand for all fucking women
I might have lost the battle

But I'll win this fucking war
I didn't feel a fucking thing
I fucking hate you with every fiber of my being
I'll leave you sinking
Cut up and drinking
What the fuck are you thinking?
Careless help less little man
I've been a soldier since my life began
I'm a fucking psycho
But that's quite alright though
I'm lighting this mother fucker up
I'm not a wimping cub
I will fucking annihilate you
I didn't shake in my boots
I fucking faced you
I will put my fucking lighter in the air
You won't see me cus of all the smoke
Look at all the pain you caused me
I am made by pains, hurt and betrayal
I will battle threw it all
Your the one that's going to fall
I don't want another fucking sorry
Fuck all your bullshit
Fuck you!

You threaten me

I say I can't hear you

I don't fear you

You couldn't see me

You didn't see the army at my back

I don't give a fuck

You never isolated me like you thought

You cut me off from nothing

So just stop ya playing

I'll leave you fucking burning

I'm burning this fucking rope

I'm so close the winning goal

I will always have hope

See you again mother fucker

Careless helpless little man

Chris the love of my life

His name is Chris,
He's been with me all threw this,
All I do is run away because I think the grass is greener on the other side,
He's always been there by my side,
It's greener where you water it,
I won't give up on him,
He helps me to swim,
He's the one my heart calls upon,
He's been there threw every tear,
He's been there every single year,
He keeps me above the water,
He is my lover,
The very thing I've been looking for has been there the entire time,
With him by my side I'll be fine,
To you I'll always be true,
Me and you eh? who knew?
Put your arms around me and tell me everything's okay,
There's so many things I can't say,

My heart flutters everyday,

I know every so often I stray,

We always find our way back together again,

We always laugh and say here we are again,

I am not afraid,

Please say you have got me and you’re never going to leave,

In us I believe,

Darling won't you hold my hand,

Will you understand?

There's no denying,

With you I’m not hiding,

I know I am not alone,

I don't want to break,

With you I’m not fake,

He's helped me and seen me threw,

He’s been by my side for the last five years,

He's been there to wipe away my tears.

Contemplate

I contemplate suicide, nobody knows the secrets I hide,
I don't want to be left behind, myself I now find,
I will always fight, that's the thing I'll do right,
I'm used to your kind, Mental poison in my veins,
I'll stay in my own lanes, I'm breaking free from my chains,
For myself I will shine, this life is mine,
I'll blind your eyes, I dream of summer bays,
People are cutting my rope so it frays,
I ask myself who I am, I think of my Nan,
I've been running since my life began,
You don't know who I am, my hands are starting to slip,
My heart feels this drip, Hang on let me adjust my grip,
I won't abandon this ship, I'm in this total eclipse,
My reaction you won't be able to predict,
I've been looking in the mirror,
I've been raised in terror,
Don't try me I'll leave in horror,

I'll leave you with a boner,

Then I’ll leave you to be a loner,

You won't get your closure,

You I will torture, I'll invade your mind,

Then I will walk away and leave you behind,

I stare at my reflection with admiration,

I clench my teeth, nobody knows these scars underneath,

Fuck around and I’ll stick it to your throat,

I'll leave you gagging for breath,

Do I really believe in a life after this?

I can hear the hiss,

Of all the people trying to bring me down,

Fuck you! You won't make me drown,

Hang on let me straighten my crown,

Fuck I contemplate, You I’ll deflate,

In my life I rotate, I will stand and smile at devils gate,

He will welcome me home with open arms.

Do you know

Do you know what it feels like to be kicked, Do you know what it feels like to be punched,
It feels like I've been pushed around, I've been put down, I feel so insecure,
Damn! I can't stay strong anymore, Welcome to my show, do you know I'm feeling lost and alone,
With nowhere to call home, I'm in this never ending bubble, I'm always in trouble,
I'm barely breathing, I'm so tired of my pretending, and all I want is a happy ending,
The darkness is dawning, I feel Asif I'm drowning, and it's too dark to see,
I'm sure I've reached the end, all I ever wanted is a friend,
This noise is deafening, I'm under the weights of expectations,
Do you know what it feels like to never be enough, this battle is so tough?
I've been messing up lately, I am giving up nightly,
Self-sabotage is an old friend of mine, I sit in my

room and contemplate of all the ways I could die,
I just lay there and stare at the sky, I will not ask why,
The stuff I done has been dumb, damn! I feel so numb,
I've made many a mistakes, I need to press the brakes,
Do you know what this feels like?

Don't

Don't make a choice for them, Make a choice for you,
For my own ambitions, I'm driving away you're temptations,
I won't validate my feelings to you, I choose me, my mind and my future,
I'll look inside me and I will nurture, I will look at me and be proud,
I won't shy away from my reflection, Shit! I need a new direction,
I won't let you dictate my reaction, I'm building my own empire,
I'm filled with so much fire, God! You I despise, I don't like you,
My own life I will live, Look how far I've come, yes I've fallen,
And hit the ground with a thud, I just sit here and play in the mud,
I'll build piece by piece, I look now for inner peace, and I take a breath and a sigh of relief,
I'm on my own path, I won't let you have a hold

over me, I'll just say fuck em and be me,
I make a choice and I choose me, I'm a lost, damaged beautiful angel, I choose me
I'll soar threw the clouds, I hold onto me, only me can keep me safe,
God! How do I escape this place, me you under estimate,
That's where you went wrong, in this world I do belong,
You under estimated me I'm a lot stronger than you think,
Fuck you! Have another drink or another pill, I know you will,
I feel nothing more for you, if anything I feel sorry for you,
You'll never know love, friendship or bravery oh dear! Is this getting to hazy for you?
What the hell is my fate which path do I take,
I choose me and my future that's what I choose,
That's the thought I keep close, I'm over you for sure,
Don't bring me your shit, It's not my fault, don't bring me you're assault,
Don't even try and make me feel guilty, you tried

to break the pieces of my mind,
Now myself I have to try and find, so don't even try and break me in two,
Fuck you! You don't have a clue, so go ahead and do what you do best,
Just give it a rest, here we go again with your mind games,
I guess you don’t like the flames, you need a restraint,
My heart you won't stain, you think you broke my heart,
Please you're so average, I was already a savage, I don't need all of your baggage,
I was used to abuse from a young age so I already knew the world was a dangerous place,
I showed you my resilience, you won't keep me silent, why did you have to be so violent,
You really think you're the only loss that I faced,
I can handle the shit you’re throwing, you’re no one worth knowing,
You brought this on yourself so go ahead and hang yourself, so just fucking don't, Get off the phone and leave me the fuck alone,
You’re the one that's going to be lost and alone.

Electric

I wish I didn’t have this shitty tattoo to remind me of you,

Guess that's love and it's fucked me up,

Who do these people think they are?

Tearing down my heart, ripping me apart,

My poetry is a work of art,

Fuck am I just over feeling,

I'm just trying to stay afloat,

Just floating in this boat,

Can I find a way to co-exist with my demons,

Why do I get treated this way?

When will I be okay?

Should I just call it quits?

Fuck that I can't give up on this,

Was I so out of line?

Don't walk away, Stay,

Pain shooting threw me like electric,

Crying is so fucking pathetic,

I'm angry, depressed and I’m mad,

Reminiscing over the good days we had,

Was I really that bad?

What's the point of all this,

Can I just start over now?

I'm reaching my hands out in the darkness,

I'm not giving up,

I can feel this pain shooting threw me like fucking electric.

Empty shell

Do you know it's like to be this empty shell of a person of the thing you made me into?
I look to god to see me threw, I was made into everything you wanted, All the times I was abandoned,
No sense of the person I'm meant to be, I look now to set myself free, I don't know who I am fuck my mum and my family,
Yet again I'm silenced my life remains unbalanced, I'm constantly on this ever tightening rope, All I needed was a ray of hope,
Instead of this never ending slope, I'm going downhill, all the things you said are true, and Yet again I am shed,
I feel sick from this whiplash, I keep replaying all of my past, I just get met with the words of you should've known better,
How can I when I was still a child, trying to run free and wild, I didn't get to choose or feel the world around me,
So much more I have to prove, I kept silent to

protect you but who protects me from this cycle, Damn!!
I feel so cold, I didn't get a chance to choose who I was or what my life was going to be, All this hurt is all that I see,
Nobody understands the demons I face, I try to rest in a safe place but how do I protect myself from people in masks,
Pretending to care, this is so unfair, I can hear my heart beating so fast, in this cycle that feels all so familiar,
It feels safe because of what I'm used to, I give the excuse of it's okay I'm used to it, How do I break free from this empty person, I need to learn the lesson of this empty shell, I am not yet where I need to be or where I need to go,
I have no destination or direction but all I know is I need to fill up this empty shell with so much fire, I'm alive, I need to fill up this god forsaken well, my story I still have yet to tell, I'm filled with so much sorrow
I still wake up tomorrow, with my energy I get up and keep moving, Myself I won't be losing,
I'm filling up this empty shell with so much light

because I'm not losing this fight,

I'll be alright, my heart I'll keep inside, how do I feel up this empty vessel, that remains the question.

Energy

Like a giddy kid she said, So many things going off in my head,
Don't give me the surface shit I'm here for the underworld of this mother fucker!
You're the one I'll leave in the gutter, I'm a functional member of society,
We're all just a minority, just a little sobriety,
I'm building in silence so people don't know what to attack,
Don't try and test me I'll just eat you and call it a snack,
I'm channeling my energy, keeping it into myself,
Generated by myself, I'm putting love back into myself,
I derailed the fuck it train, I'm working in real time,
Keep going I'm onto a winner, Betray me and I'll eat you for dinner,
I'm filled with so much passion, Fuck that wanker called depression,
I don't break easy anymore, No not me, whatever

people throw at me I’ll use as fuel,
Oh fuck! Shit just got real, So much more work I have left to do,
So many words still to be written, I'm not no purring kitten,
I'm a tiger waiting to pounce, I'll destroy you without making a sound,
I'm operating so please be cautious, I'll leave you nauseous,
I'm flawless, in this life I’ll be victorious,
I wouldn’t want to see you burn,
My trust you gotta earn,
I'm summing up my life with well shit that didn’t go as planned.

Fuck you

You don't know what it's like to be so messed up that you hope that you die,

When you're over your life and you know that you might put a knife to your throat as you cry,

I just wanted to die. But I chose to survive because I think I could focus and try more,

I don't wanna die from emotions I hide, you couldn't care that I'm broken inside,

You just poked and provoked till the moment's arrived, you came in my knickers and posted them to my mum,

All I wanted to do is run, I was so over my life that you made me want to die.

If I got the chance to speak to you, I'd ask you, why you said I should die, and go join my Nan and my nephew, if only you knew. Why did you say my brother abused me?

Why did you make up all these lies, why did you try and get me to stay I tried to hold on every day,

I don't think you understand what you did to me, or maybe you did know but didn't care,

How can you be so unfair, when asked how I felt about this I have no words,
Phoning crisis lines, just to stay alive.
This I will survive how did it come to this? To think that I felt at the beginning of all this, it wasn't my fault,
To finch every time my phone goes off, the fact you have been following me, just set me free and let me be me. Do the right thing for once and let me go, so much more I would want to say to you, but know this we are over and I'm over my life.
You make me sick, you're a "crazy prick",
I don't want my mum to look at me like I'm nothing but a "nutter", but your making stuff up about my brother. Can I just have a moment of peace?
I'm afraid to quit I choose to survive. You sent me pictures with a noose on a beam, now you're locked up is a relief. Maybe now I can have some peace,
I was in a refuge and kept thinking what if I just put this bag over my head I will suffocate,
What if I jump out this window, what if I run into the road?

What if I just smash this glass bottle and slit my throat, what if I just take these tablets, or just simply slit my wrists. Replying to you I've resisted, why you had to be so persistent, you're putting me in isolation,

You caused me so much suffering, when all I showed you was devotion, all this you did to me, no more torment. Even when I told you to stop, you didn't you went through every family member and my friends,

My life you made me want to end, told you we were through, if only you knew the impact you have had,

Just look at the way you act, all the times you messed up the pieces of my mind,

Now I have to try and find who I am and you I'll leave behind, but you made me just want to die.

Now it's my time to say "fuck you" and "goodbye".

Fading away

I can't remember the sound of your voice,

I can't remember what you look like,

I can't remember any memories we shared,

Maybe it's because you never cared,

Or just maybe I was never really in love,

You left my heart with bruises, stained and broken,

I was left alone in the dark, I can't remember

No matter how hard I try, I suppose it's because you left me to cry,

How did I get so torn, Your full of deceit and lies,

Away from you I now fly, I fly so high in the sky,

I'm finding myself every day, I'm releasing everything I want to say,

Every day you fade away, I have nothing more to say,

The place you once had in my heart has now departed,

Your place has now been taken by love for myself,

I say everything I want to say right here in these pages,

You no longer have your places,

Every day you fade away,

Your fading away day by day you fade away.

Free fall

I'm in free fall, do I just risk it all,
Spending money on counselling,
To try and get over it eventually,
All my life it's been fucking with me mentally,
Personality disorder she said,
Maybe I am fucked in the head,
I hope I can find away,
Guess that's apart of my disorder,
Acting on impulse, Shit!
Maybe I need a new fuse,
I refuse to lose, I'm in free fall,
it's getting cold out here,
Damn! I know my demons well,
My story I still have yet to tell,
My tears could fill up a well,
I'm my mother's daughter,
I don't need my father,
Some days won't come easy,
This world is mine for the taking,
Fuck it! I don't need saving,
You better believe it,

Success is my only option,

As long as my fire is burning,

Got to keep my life turning,

Got to keep on winning,

I'm so close to my happily ever after,

I need to fill my head with laughter,

Why do you need to creep in my dome?

Why can't you just leave me alone?

Can I just have a moment of peace?

Fuck it! I'm just in free fall.

Fuck it

I can't do this anymore, nothing ever changes,
I carry on the basis I can face this,
I'm in this never ending train,
I'm forever afraid, my heart I just can't contain,
All I know is this cycle of abuse,
All I ever do is just get used,
All the nights I sit and cry, I'm sick of asking myself why,
Fuck it that's just me and I'll give it another try,
Fuck I just wanna die, I try to let this shit go,
Whatever I'm alive for I just don't know,
Nothing gets better, it's been that way for ages,
I wanna be alone, I have no place to call home,
I feel so cold, all I ever do is just grow old,
I'm so tired from feeling the same,
I just wanna numb the feels,
I look for an answer at the bottom of a bottle,
My neck I just wanna throttle,
Don't hold me because I'm falling back down,
I wouldn't want to see you hit the ground,
You found my heart in the lost and found,

The scars follow me around,

I wake up every morning with my head in a daze,

I'm not sure if I should say this,

I'll say it anyway,

Everyone is trying to tell me I’m going threw a phase,

It's not a fucking phase I just wanna feel okay,

I can't hold on anymore,

I can't do this anymore,

I struggle with this bullshit everyday,

My demons simultaneously rage,

It suffocates me, it obliterates me,

Disintegrates me, Annihilates me,

Am I just going threw a phase,

Am I just going to an early grave?

Fuck it another day done.

Fuck the yous

Fuck the kisses, fuck the I love yous

I knew you would try to ruin my life, Thank god I'm not you're wife,

Fuck the pieces of my mind you fucked with,

I know you hate me but I hate you more,

I'm running out the door, You won't leave me shattered on the floor,

FUCK you're gas lighting, Fuck you for making me question my own thinking,

Fuck you for making me question my own reality,

Fuck you for making me question my own feelings,

I fucking hate you with every fiber of my being,

Fuck you for fucking with my emotions,

Fuck you're manipulation,

Sorry my bad for making you mad,

Sorry for loving you my bad,

Fuck you for making me disorientated,

Fuck you for making me depressed,

Fuck you for leading me a stray,

Fuck you and your false narrative,

Fuck you for being so addictive,
Fuck all the names you called me,
Just because I wasn’t the person you needed me to be,
Just fucking leave me alone,
Stop creeping in my dome,
Stop trying to break me,
Fuck you for trying to break me,
Fuck you,
Your a cunt,
I know to my friends I put up a frunt,
I'm focusing on spreading awareness for domestic violence, i'll show you my resilience,
Nobody should be afraid,
I replay all the words you've ever said,
I count the amount of times you made me wish I was dead,
All the times you fucked with my head,
Fuck you!! Fuck all the times you tried to make me react,
To myself I now make a pact,
To never put myself in this position again,
I won't quit, you don't mean shit,
Yeah! Fuck you and all your I love yous

I walk alone

I walk alone I walk this lonely road, It's the only road I've ever known,
I keep walking with no direction, Walking is my only destination,
My mind plays tricks on me, Or am I just been paranoid,
I'm living in this endless void, I ask my angels to look after me,
I'm trying to be me, I pray to god to take this pain away, making it threw just one more day,
All these hands try to grab me, that's so predictable,
I'm strong and I am able and worth it all, I'm being prepared for what's to come,
So when is everything going to be said and done,
I know I had the time of my life,
For now I walk alone along this lonely road, the only road I've ever known,
I'm crying all the time but I'm taking back my life,
I'm relighting my flame,
I will never be the same, I'll climb that mountain

and I’ll be strong,
When you come around I know my power will have been found,
My fire you won't diminish, My light you won't extinguish,
I laugh at all my past, I learnt all the things I needed to know,
It's my time now so I need to let it all go,
As for now I walk this lonely road.

I woke up

I woke up this morning, first step get up, Make a coffee,
Life's so frothy, don’t be so cocky, I had a call from my mum,
She said I won't let that doctor stick their finger up my bum,
She's so funny, her nose is always runny, she’s a pickled onion,
The most stress of today was not being able to cut up an onion,
All I had was a butter knife, you’re not worth life,
I'm full of layers, I have layers of people protecting me,
So I’m not the one who's alone, I sit typing in my phone,
So I woke up this morning, I had freedom to do what I want,
To my family I don't put up a frunt, I walked into a room,
I forgot why I went in there, this my safe haven,
I'm flying now like a raven, I am loved, and I am

enough,

I will always bounce back, I have a strong comeback game,

I'm so strong, I just want to dance and sing a song,

My mum always used to talk about a dark room,

For you I have no more room, My nan coming running,

When my brother used his feet to fling my mum in the air,

My Nan came running and says Mandy you could've broke you're back,

I'm resting now in my lair, so I woke up this morning,

I realized my self-worth, you're not worth being on this earth,

When I asked who would miss you I was met with no one,

When I asked who would miss me I was met with everyone,

You're going to be the lonely one, you have no empathy,

You'll be forever empty, Family is something you lack,

You just need a fucking smack! This is my life,

I want to dance and sing in the sun,

When all this is said and done,

I'm so glad I ran, you will never understand,

Don't you try to bring me down?

Because you're the one that will drown,

So I woke up this morning and realized I won.

In their words

She's the girl with the great sense of humour,
She's the girl with strong will power,
She's the girl with the positive attitude,
She's the girl who's cute,
She's the girl who's impulsive,
She's the brave girl,
She's the girl with the caring nature,
She's the girl that's the ray of sunshine,
She's the girl that's resilient,
She's the girl with the words,
She's the girl with the strength,
She's the girl who says give it a whazz,
She's the girl with the zesty attitude,
She's the girl with the heartwarming smile,
She's the girl with the courage,
She's the girl who's more than an outsider,
She's the girl with the best cuddles,
She's the girl with all the wants,
She's the girl with the determination,
She's the girl who's strong,
She's the stubborn girl,

She's the girl who gets up and tries again,
She's the girl with the brilliant laugh,
She's the smoke till we die right,
She's the let's get high type,
She's the take on a challenge,
These are all the words of the people closest to me,
That's the girl I will be.

Inner child

It’s okay to be broken and let it all out, I know you want to shout, let it all out, All the words you've left unspoken,
You can whisper them to me child, tell me all you need to say,
Cry inner child, don’t worry I’ll stick around for a awhile,
Cry inner child, Here is a safe place, you’re not out of place,
Burry your face, I know you had to go threw hell,
Your story you can tell me, Wash away your pain,
Go right ahead inner child, Cry little child,
I know you didn’t get a chance to be wild,
Sleep all your demons away child,
Let you tears roll of your face,
I know the loss you’ve face, Cry child,
Let's escape together, be strong child,
Be strong now more than ever, this won't last forever,
I know your burden child, I know it's been too big to bear,

Cry little child, Hold my hand child

I'll be your friend, I'll meet you there,

I know your life has been unfair,

Soon you will feel freedom,

You don’t have to feel strong forever, it’s okay child,

It’s okay child let your guard down,

I won’t let you down, Cry child,

I know you’ve tried to hold on for way to long,

In your tears the answer can be found, be proud child,

Little child you'll be okay,

I will walk with you, I’ll walk here beside you,

Tell me all you need to say, let’s face another day,

Cry little child, Rest your head,

Take my hand and come with me,

I'll carry you, you aren't alone inner child

Let’s fight

I know many people will relate to this, all the people that took the piss,

Let's fight for we believe is right,

Let's take our light and light up the night,

Let's fight for our beliefs, let’s fight our traits,

All those voices inside our heads wishing we was dead,

Get that out of your head, let’s fight,

Whatever weather cold or warm, living in this crazy storm?

Take my hand and let's take a stand and rise unafraid,

Trying to do the best for your children knowing their one in a million,

We're done living a life we can no longer fake,

Let's climb that mountain and live a life we can maintain,

Men and women suffer in silence,

I'm breaking the stigma against domestic violence,

You can beat us, Shame us, Blame us, Manipulate

us, Gaslight us, but you will never break us, They gave us butterflies,
As time went by we got sick of all their lies,
Living in a refuge but losing the fight we refuse,
Us they will no longer use, you keep asking to get you're angel wings, why when we have so many special things, listening to music to take us away,
Praying to make it threw another day,
Tell me why you can't try, I know we all sit silently and cry,
I know you ask the same question of why,
I know they wouldn't let us leave but all you needed was to believe,
So I have some things to say, don't worry tomorrow is another day,
The assault isn't your fault, you was afraid,
You say where did I go wrong, don't worry we all belong,
Take a breath and be strong,
We can beat this together,
We are all children of the earth,
We will never be broken, one breath,
We are men and women of the world,
We fight together! Hand in hand together.

Listen to my heart

I'm listening to my heart,

I don't know where I am going, I am not lost in the dark,

You won't diminish my spark, I'm listening to my heart,

You I will out smart, I am giving my heart a restart,

I will give depression a mention,

I'm listening to my heart, it's calling for me today,

Don't be so shocked, you I deleted and blocked,

You I stopped, Stabbed and dropped,

You I out smarted, I caught you while you was parked,

Away from you I now depart, I'm listening to my heart,

Each day you fade away, Day by day you disappear,

You're the one that goes to sleep in fear,

Cry alone and shed a tear, sleeping alone with one eye open,

You're the one that's left alone and broken,

I myself now have awoken, No more of me will be stolen,
Try to hurt me and I will cause an explosion,
But today I'm listening to my heart.

Love story

You're a heart breaker, when I said I loved you I was faking,
You must have been mistaken, my heart won't be taken,
I'm learning from my mistakes, I'm wiser and older,
You won't leave me colder, you I will scolder,
Don't feed me your love story, if only,
I want all my tears back that I cried, you never tried,
You I'll leave behind, We we're so toxic,
I stopped myself from communicating with you,
Your words had me numb, how can I have been so dumb,
From you I wanted to run because the relationship was done,
The vibe was weird actually it was absurd,
I'm glad I walked away, You're not welcome to another one of my day,
I thought you was the shadow to my light,
To get away from you I fought,

You won't keep me caught, don’t give your love story,
It was all just fucking bullshit.

Me and you

I'm counting stars, broken glass,
Deafening silence, I'm trying to find my way back to myself,
I'm not that person anymore, all I want is a bit of love,
Time has flew, I want to go to where it's me and you,
You're like the air I'm breathing, you're my heart that's beating,
It's always been me and you, To you I'll always be true,
I'm swimming in the deep end, I'm always trying to get back to you,
I love it when it's me and you, we go together,
We go together like two peas in a pod, I whisper a thank you to god,
You make me feel alive, you make me feel like I can float, my heart you caught, Every time we touch my heart ignites,
You give me butterflies,
I love it when it's just me and you.

Mistake

You said it's a mistake that's no mistake, don't be fake, I sit and replay the messages,
It's the feeling of betrayal, you already set me up for the fall, For you I would have given my all,
But you won't take my soul, It doesn't matter now I'll put my phone away, I walk into tomorrow,
You're not worth my sorrow, I know this will hurt for some time but I'll be fine,
I can feel the walls closing in, Now my life can begin, I'm too drunk to even walk,
I guess you want to talk, well talk to your other personality, I'm stepping back into my reality,
I'll stay awake with myself, All you have ever given me is grief, Leaving you is such a relief,
My boxes stacked against the door, my memories hit the floor, I deserve so much more,
Myself I adore, I'm so glad we're done, You left me scared to even think you cared,
Fuck! I played the part right from the start, I'm one in a million, you're the villain,
I'm better off without you, I'll keep holding onto

myself, If only you loved me,
Yeah right, broke every promise you ever made,
Here we go again the same old argument,
Is this real or just pretend, I'm glad we came to an end, I'm not crazy,
I'm not changing any part of me, I thought it was love but I caught out your bullshit,
I have nothing more to give, none of it was a mistake, and I've made a mistake once or twice,
I've always dug myself out with blood and fire,
Congrats on your shitty life,
To think I was almost you're wife, Thank god I made it out alive, you knew what you was doing,
Fuck I'm falling, Psycho, Totally mental, why don't you leave me alone,
Why keep calling my phone, I guess you like the game, Shit do you even know you're own name,
I've got to get this off my chest and lay it to rest,
God! I've just got a little bit of regret,
You're not half the man that you think you are, I'm glad I got out of the door,
I ran so fucking far, how do I feel so good sober,
I've got a brand new attitude,
I don't need you anymore, I made it out without

breaking down, I won't cry anymore tears,
Why I believed all of your promises, I really meant well from the start,
But I guess I'm just another mistake, Glad I got out before you had anything else to take,
So have a Kit Kat and give it a fucking break!!!

My city

It’s a Tuesday morning, A rainbow lights up the sky, I can hear the bustle and hustle coming from the city,
I can hear the noise coming from the street,
Buildings big and small, Wide and tall,
The smell of McDonalds wafting up my nose,
Cars rushing to get to work on time,
People walking and bikers biking,
Signs wafting in the wind,
I love this Sheffield town,
Stones pave the streets,
Factories roaring,
Buildings in the heart of the city,
I can see a blue building where my friend nick works,
I can see the baby panda climbing up the stone
A monument,
it’s the building across from the church,
This is where I was born,
This is my Sheffield
This is my city,

Narcissist

Trust me he said, I'll never hurt you he said,
He'll never break my heart he said, He'll never desert me he said,
He showed me love at the start, He laughed as he broke my heart,
He gave me all the strings to pull myself apart,
He was the one in control, He was my free for all,
For him I gave my all,
Every time we fought he made sure I knew it was my fault,
He hovered me back in and showed me the love he showed me in the beginning,
He left me questioning my own thinking, He took over my life one step at a time,
I said to myself its okay he does it because he cares, Bullshit,
He took away my voice, I felt like loving him was my only choice,
He showed me how to hate myself, He manipulated me,
He took me away from my friends and loved ones,

From my friends he took me away, at the beginning I thought he was okay,
Cracks started showing and my sky started to become grey,
He made sure I knew I was here to stay, I couldn't get away,
I got down on my knees and I pray,
He confused me so much my mind became blurred,
He left me thinking is this what I deserved,
He brought out all my demons I kept so well hid,
I hated the life I lived,
I needed to escape from this catastrophe,
He broke me down, I try to get myself back to the person I once was,
I'm weak, Tired and no strength found,
Cold heart left shattered on the ground,
I'm trying to come back from the mess that he made,
To him this was all just a game, He so well played,
Great! I did it I finally escaped,
He laughed at all my broken pieces,
That I tumbled clumsily and I try to put back together,

I know he is near, I live in fear, I have scars on my heart,
From where he pulled me apart, these scars follow me around,
They follow me around, I'm still trying to pick myself up, up of the ground.

New Beginnings

This life is mine for the taking, My story is only just beginning,
I'm going to be a super star, I've come so far,
I'm so proud of everything that I am,
I'm only just getting started,
I'm the one that will leave you broken hearted,
I'm showing all my haters wrong,
In this world I do belong,
You shouldn't fear my words, you should fear my silence,
I'm spreading awareness for domestic violence,
If you're stupid enough to betray my trust, you better get ready to run,
Destroying you will be fun, I'll leave you in a pile of dust,
So try again if you must,
Anyone who tries to bring me down I hope you're ready to drown,
I'm amazing, I don't need saving, I'm not a damsel in distress,
In my life I'll have success, I've been born again

from the ashes,

I'm rising within the flames, as I lay here in my slumber, I am resting,

In myself I'm investing, when I open my eyes the whole world will hear me roar,

So don't come for me anymore, I know each one of my demons by name,

Even Satan himself is afraid, I've been threw the pits of hell,

I'm breaking free from my cell, I'm stepping into the other side,

I won't hide, I'm my own savior, So I don't need you favors,

I'm not giving up, I'll be the person I'm destined to be,

I'll set myself free, I know no one else might not believe in me,

I'm not giving up, No not me, this is my new beginning,

So any one trying to bring me down,

What the fuck are you thinking?..

New Chapter

In my life I'm opening a new chapter,
Leaving my old pages to grow dusty,
Putting my past to rest, The old chapter is not who I am now,
I'm leaving my old story behind,
I'm no longer giving my past my attention,
I'm no longer giving it my participation,
I don't fear my past, I won't fear it,
I'll just write another chapter,
Leaving the ink stained pages behind,
The heartbreak I once had is now fading into the shadow,
I'm stepping away from what I know,
My life I'm bringing a new,
To myself i'll always be true,
This is my new chapter,
Today I am calm, Today I have calmed myself,
I'll leave my pages with holes in them,
I wiped away my tears and I picked myself back up,
I'll leave my battered heart, Bruised soul,

I'll leave my twisted mind in the pages of this book,

I will put it away, I'll leave it under lock,

I'll throw the key away,

I'm putting my book away today,

Occasionally I take it out and re read it,

To take from it another lesson,

I now organize it and put it in places,

I now deal with my burden,

I learn my lesson from my torn and ripped pages,

I now take the ink of my chest,

I now lay it to rest,

Today I open my new chapter and I put my book away today.

Outsider

I've been made an outsider in my own family,
Is this just now my reality, being told it's my fault?
I feel so cold, how is my own family turning against me,
I don't know the person I'm supposed to be,
I feel like a stranger in my own skin,
You are all having a go at me so yet again he will win,
Telling me I should've known better, how can I,
I was still a child, I've never had any identity,
All I've ever done is shown you empathy,
Even though I gave and gave and now I'm empty,
I was never allowed to grieve, it's me this is happening too,
I had no place to go, What did I do all this for,,
You won't accepted you all failed,
You say it's my fault for going back,
I went back to protect you all, I took the fall,
How can I carry on when I did everything for you all?
What about me?

What about the child me?

What about the teenage me?

What about the adult me ?

What about the drained me?

What about the dead me ?

Don't cry at my funeral, You're not bothered,

I'm here now and you all never bother,

your not bothered now while I'm alive,

Fuck this life, You've never seen any of it,

I guess you don't like the thought of it,

Fuck all this shit,

All my life all I've known is abuse,

Losing the battle I refuse,

I won't lose,

I've always been the black sheep of the family,

Myself I now make a priority,

I guess I'm just an outsider

Over

I'm just fine now it's over,

Hang on let me find my composure,

I can hear your melody, You was my remedy,

You left me to bleed internally,

My life is better without you,

Did you think I'd crumble?

Hating on me I'm ready to rumble,

Did you think I'd break down and cry?

I'm a warrior, I won't break down,

No not me, Did you think I'd just lay down and die?

Do you think its okay to call me a hoe? No I don't think so,

I'm stronger than you'll ever know, I'll destroy you,

Don't burn your fingers on my flames,

Shut the fucking door on your way out.

People

I see people just walking past, I’m screaming but no one's listening,
All I can hear is that deafening echo of all the words they've ever said,
All the times you all made me cry, thinking it's all my fault, you all had the choice of hurting me and yet you all still did it, you all knew the brunt of the impact,
loving myself now is a proven fact, as I sit here as people are strolling past,
I put my ear to the ground, all I can hear is silence and the beating of my heart,
I look around I see people rushing in all different directions, we're all just trying
to get threw each day, All heading in a different way, If only one would stop and ask are you okay,
I sit here staring at my phone, I'm hearing nothing but the sound of your lost and alone, I hold on barely breathing,
I'm so close to breaking, nobody can hear the screams of my soul,

I continue to sit here watching people go about their day, I contemplate if I was to disappear would
anyone remember me, Would anyone even care, I sit here with tears in my eyes,
I look and I'll say I'm fine all said with a smile, I'll sit here with myself for a while, ill sat here watching these people rushing on by.

Pretend

I won't pretend to understand why we came to an end, I won't pretend this doesn't hurt,
My healing doesn't need to be graceful, None the less I will heal,
No more of me will you steal, I need to forgive myself for going threw yet again,
You caused me so much pain, So many things left unsaid but that's quite alright,
I'll pack up my heart and I'll scream into the night,
I won't pretend to understand,
I won't pretend not to cry, I won't pretend I don't have questions of why,
Everything you said has been a lie, I will put my pieces back together,
I might have got lost along the way, You're not welcome to another day,
I have nothing more to say, I need to be strong now more than ever,
I won't pretend not to feel this, I'll lick the bruises on my heart,
I'll give myself a brand new start, I'll keep on

moving, and I’ll keep pushing forward,

I can't go back, My energy I now reserve, Myself is the most I deserved,

I'll just smile and wave you goodbye, I'll just carry on walking,

But I won't pretend, I deserved so much more than this,

Speaking to you I’ll give a miss, I keep asking myself is it my imagination,

I'm setting myself a little destination, Never the less I can't pretend of why,

We came to an end.

PTSD

PTSD its the funny little voice in the back of your mind,
the furious flashbacks, The silent voice to throw you off track,
It's a funny thing I didn't employ, My mind you set to destroy,
You leave me annoyed, My mind you exploit, Shit! I've hit the check point,
It's the creeping nightmares, staring at the stars,
It's not feeling safe, I hope I can find away to say all I need to say,
It's the silent voice whispering so silently in my ears,
It's bringing up all my fears, It's making me kneel on all fours,
It's making me anxious, Shit! Being in my brain is disastrous,
It's exploiting all my traumas, It's bringing me endless dramas,
Days spent just in my pajamas, I keep myself guarded with precautions,

If your brain is gone stay awake with me,
I know your feelings have gone, You're causing me to be disturbed,
My ears have been burned, All these events that occurred,
My demons have emerged, it's a funny thing I need to unlearn,
It's a funny little thing called ptsd

Purpose

You wanted to see me break, Big mistake,

You won't see me fall, I'll just rise and give it my all,

You won't take my soul, Myself I forgive,

I'll just stand up even taller, I'm now wiser and older,

I'm a soldier, Come with me,

I'm going to live the life I was always destined to live,

Better days are coming for me, Myself I believe in,

My story is not yet over, I've grown strong,

I’ve learnt how to get along, I'll just put on my armor,

I'll charge, No more expectations, I'm burning every bridge,

That doesn’t lead to a better me,

I know now who I’m supposed to be,

Today I woke up and had a sense of purpose,

Finding my secret pleasure, Redirecting my entire life,

I will thrive, I will survive, This is now my time,

To hit the reset button and begin to live again,

To have new focus, This is the universe calling me home,

This is it, It's now done, it’s now over,

Now my life I can begin, I'm shifting all my love into myself,

Trying to get somewhere, I'm trying my hardest,

I haven’t even started yet,

I'll never be a quitter,

My self is now my purpose.

Self Love

I accept myself as a work in progress,
I'm building myself into the person I’m dreaming to be,
It's now time to put myself first,
I now let go of all the bad times,
I now let go of all the negativity,
I'm letting myself find my creativity,
I'm walking steady, I'm now ready,
I'm reaching for the moon,
I'm sick of being stuck in this doom and gloom,
I'm telling all the voices in my head,
To go away and talk to someone else instead,
I now self-medicate,
My light I now radiate,
I won't ever stop,
The sky's the limit,
This is it,
I am now loving myself,
I have undeniable strength,
I know how to make the moon listen,
I lead the pack of the wolves,

I now feel content,

I now feel full in my heart.

She

She has fallen apart before, So this time is not any different,
She needs to stay content and have herself focus,
She needs to pull herself together,
She picks up the pieces she needs, She begins to rebuild herself like she always does,
She moves forward from her past, Her hearts beating fast, Her life needs to last,
Broken hearts and last loves are no stranger to her, The love she's been looking for has been looking for
has been under nose the entire time, Herself, She rages threw seas of discontentment many times,
She knows she faces a challenge when she chooses to love the way she does,
She gives love her all, She braces herself for the never ending fall, Loving herself is her only goal,
She doesn't do anything half way, She wouldn’t change a thing about the choices she makes,
She's made many mistakes, She never will stop believing in true love, She tries to build a brighter

future,
She never choose this path, She wasn't given any other choice, When the darkness of a broken love tries to bring her down,
She just smiles and says not today sadness, She just struggs it off, Living, laughing and loving will always be her way,
She shakes her head and turns to face the sunlight and shines, She loves with all her heart,
That's the price she pays for loving the way she does.

Should've

Hold me, Do you want to know me?
I can't predict, I'm feeling my instinct,
You wasted all my time, Fuck everything you did,
I can't stay sober, You're a loser,
You wasted all my time, I should have left that shit at hello,
I knew you never could change, You're deranged,
You break things, I should have hung up when I saw you're name,
You took it to far, it's better to be broken,
Don't fall to fast, I should have saved myself from this pain,
I should have just hung up when I saw your fucking name.

Social network

Isn't it funny to use social media to stay connected,
When in reality we're all disconnected,
Can anybody really know they know the people that's on their social media page,
Isn't it strange, Where all just trying to get somewhere,
Showing others we care, The little whispers in the world,
Being your friend I confirmed, it's a weird thing called social network,
All sharing our work, All sitting staring at our phones while the real moments slip away,
Conversations becoming text messages, Pictures posted of people having the best times,
Sitting a room full of people, Yet staring at the thing we call a phone,
It's a funny thing called social network, Isn't it funny to use social media to stay connected,
When in reality we're all disconnected.

Storm clouds

I can feel a storm raging within, I can feel myself slowly getting better,
Day by day I get stronger, I'm finding my voice,
The greyness is starting to disappear and the sky is becoming blue,
The cracks on my heart are starting to fade into nothing but a scar,
I'm starting to feel confident in my own skin,
I now absorb all the pain, I now deal with my struggles,
I can feel the storm raging within,
All of you no longer have power over me,
I am now free, I'm cutting of everything that doesn't serve my purpose,
I am being me, I am no longer this scared little girl,
I'm no longer afraid of my own shadow,
If any one tries to bring me down,
I'll engulf them in my tornado,
I can feel the storm raging within.

Surrender

I won't surrender, I know challenges try to bring me down but I won't surrender,
I never set out to be strong or brave, Myself I will save,
I tell my haters to behave, In myself I now engage,
I was never given another option, I prefer making love not being at war,
Myself I now restore, No one can hurt me anymore, I'll never surrender,
I'll never surrender my soul to reach my goal,
I've made my share of mistakes, wrong turns and bad love choices,
I won't surrender my values, I never asked why, I found my way threw the struggle,
I have warrior spirit, I'll be fine, I have been searching for peace,
I never question the timings of life,
I pick myself up and continue living threw the pain,
I put myself back together again,
Each time stronger and better than before,

My life chills me to the core,
I'm more than a warrior, I'm more than a survivor,
I always keep my fire burning, I have a future full of possibilities,
I'm the light in the darkness, I'm my own destiny,
My time is now, I won't surrender, I will show the world what I've got,
I'll eventually find my way home, I'm finally at peace,
The only person I have to answer to is myself,
I believe in myself threw it all, I had to meet the devil to know his name,
My life is such a shame, I've been threw shit I didn't deserve,
Myself I now preserve, I now take a step back and observe,
No more haunting, No more hurting,
Myself I'm now supporting, Myself I'm now rewarding,
I will not surrender,
Me surrender never!!

The night time routine

Ahh the night time routine, Deciding whether to have a bath or shower,
To wash the troubles of the day away,
whether that's been at work or being busy doing nothing at all,
Like I do most days, I do the same shit most days,
Any way where was I? Ahh yes the night time routine,
I prefer a bath to soak the day away,
Going into hot water and feeling the troubles of the day,
Going threw in your mind all your worries and all your little secrets,
The things that keep you up most nights,
There's something special about submerging your head under the water,
Hearing your heart beating, Ahh its a great feeling,
Feeling the bubbles against your body, Pure bliss,
Shaving your legs and other bits,
There's nothing better than washing your troubles

away,

There's nothing better than feeling fresh and clean,

Getting into bed,

Feeling the softness of the sheets,

Resting your head,

Resting your head up in bed,

Slowly closing your eyes,

Slowly drifting away,

Ahh the night time routine.

Tired

I am to tired to keep on fighting or simply taking medication just for a simple sedation,
Or is this just another delusion, It's not the kind of tired where you simply sleep and feel better,
No this is another type of tired, No matter how much I rest my eyes I simply can not drift,
I hope you never understand this type of tired, It's fighting to wake up,
Fighting to go to sleep, Not being able to sleep is a constant exhaustion,
To keep replying moments in your mind, To not be motivated, To even get up,
You're body aches and you're mind is screaming just for a bit of silence,
To get back to you with a smile, Picking yourself up and putting yourself together again,
Tired of being put down, I'm put down by the people closest too,
The ones who claim to love me, Tired from the blame just because I am a flame,
Tired from just feeling the same, Doesn't mean

I’m going to die,

I just get back up and give it another try, I try once more to rest my eyes,

Even a simple task seems to much, I'm running from dusk till dawn,

I'll close my eyes once more if I must,

But no it's not a simple kind of tired.

Unapologetic

I will not apologies for being this way
You made me this way
It's fucked up you tried to
Hit me with your strategy
Stop fucking me with your brutality
Stop your scrutiny
I'm my own priority
But guess yet again I'm a minority
Your still out here trying to fuck with me mentally
I will show you what I'm made of
You will be the one running away with your tail cowering in between your legs
Crying to the guards
This is fucking absurd
I keep telling you don't underestimate me
I am free
Your locked away
Won't let you out
I will not apologies for being this way
You made me this way
I leave you in ashes on the ground

I keep saying didn’t you hear what I said

I'll leave you burying your head

Your going to wish you was dead

Eh? Bet your wishing now you did tie that rope around your neck

My name is fucking beck

So fuck of back

I'm unapologetic as fuck

I'm fucking coming for you.

You better be fucking ready

I’m moving steady

Moving swift

You will feel my drift

Don't be so fucking cocky

I will not apologies for being this way

You made me this way

You'll go back to the hell you came from

You are fucking scum

Worthless piece of shit

Your going to feel the force of my hit

You I will split

I must admit

I'll leave you lit

You’ve got no hope

I'm pulling this rope

I'm over that

I'm never come back

I'm not going back to hell

I've got aggression

I hit you with precision

Court is now in session

So save your breath

I'll leave you choking

Stop ya chatting

You've got no hope

Don't play with the fire

Don't be so surprised

I'll leave you vandalized

Even as a child I shined bright

Even as a child I put up a fight

Even now as an adult I still share my light

You'll feel the sting of my coldness

I can feel these storm clouds

Can it just slow down

I don't think your going to get very far

I'll beat you to death

I'll fight you with every breath

You will fall

You will break

Make no mistake

I won't stop trying

I won't go down without fighting

I'm unapologetic

I will not apologies for being this way

You made me this way

Under water

It feels like I’m drowning, something inside me is stirring, I am suffocating in this never ending prison,

I release my breath and try to look underneath, I can't see threw the water, I’m so frightened,

I need to see what's below, I breathe out slow, I can't hear anything but mumbled shouts and prayers,

No one ever listens in a place like this, it’s not peaceful under water, I can hear the water's hiss,

I'm left with the choice of holding on or floating up this never ending abyss,

I stay still holding my breath, My demons come out and play,

I often ponder if I should have ended have ended it all before it all went down hill,

The world would still be the same disfigured mess, The only difference would be one less soul trapped in cage, We're unable to dream of a place outside of this hell,

We're all trapped afraid and damaged, All sitting

still holding our breath,

We're all waiting for release into open airs,

Waiting for a thing never to come,

As the waves loom I hold my breath, With a crash

I follow the waves out of this never ending prison.

Unsaid

So many words left unsaid, But they will remain in my head,

So many things I wish I could have said to you,

But your memories see me threw,

I wish I could see you one more time,

To tell you about all about my life,

I'll be broken over words unsaid,

You I remember, I'll carry you like a fire in my heart,

I'm in too deep, I let this out and weep,

All these things I didn’t say,

I think of you all every day,

I whisper them to you, Your my guiding star,

I think of you and shed a tear,

I'm spreading big waves, My path I will pave,

My voice begins to brake,

I know this will hurt for some time,

I know I’ll be fine,

I'll carry you like a fire in my heart,

I'll sit here with you for awhile,

I keep holding on but it's forever dark,

The memorial bench at Stannington Park,

Poor little Ezra, I'll dance in his fiesta,

I think of you, My poor uncle mark,

I wish I could see you one more time and have a drink with you,

My auntie Janet, Sometimes I feel like I'm on another planet,

I always think of my nan, Every year drinking baileys,

Even though we don't like it,

With you for awhile I will sit,

So many people I lost along the way,

I think of you all everyday,

So many words left unspoken,

I'm always thinking of you,

I live on threw you,

I'll carry you like a fire in my heart.

Unstoppable

It's not until you fall down that your dreams become possible,
I am now unstoppable, I'm beautiful,
My dreams are now possible, I am creating a revolution,
I wear all my traumas like diamonds,
I am one of the dangerous ones,
I am wiping away my tears before they fall of my cheeks,
I am unstoppable, I've healed myself more times than you can imagine,
Don't mistake my soul for a quite one, I'm just contemplating my next move,
Your only seeing the casing, You don't see the storm that rages within,
I'm cleansing myself of all my sins,
Now my life begins, I'm unstoppable,
My dreams are now becoming possible.

Untitled

My voice is frozen, I can't find the words, I'm all choked up,

I don't want to be another memory, My heart still aches every time I say goodbye,

Baby it hurts, So as my world fades away I would always remember us this way,

I can't hold anymore it makes no sense to me, I'll be in the place we met,

I'm not moving, You say you love me but I need to stand my ground,

I'll be waiting on the corner of the street, How do I erase you off my skin,

it’s my dreams you take, I need to let you go, Better together turned out to be better off alone,

Are you done embarrassing me, I'm kneeling at you're feet, Please stop calling me,

You hurt me so don't give me the bullshit of you love me, You're so toxic,

You're so happy destroying every fiber of my being, How do I get rid of this feeling,

Blame me for everything if you must but please

stop calling,

You require my absence to be happy, I can't love anymore,

I'm a heart break away from a terrible place not that you care,

I'm fabricated in you're story, I'm barricaded together with bandages,

All because of you, You're fading away, Our memories I just can't erase,

I'm putting on a brave face, I'm feeling the breaking of my heart,

I should've known you was poison from the start,

Why do I let you do this, You left me in pieces on your bedroom floor,

I don't want to be the one you're scars are always leaning on,

Why does this hurt so much, How did it get to this,

I go threw stages of letting you go but here you are again,

Why cause me all this pain, I'm sorry I'm so weak,

Sorry you say just doesn't cut it, Saying my love is gone is such a pretense,

My feelings are so intense, I'm loving the very thing that's killing me,

I can't conquer it, I needed fixing the most, I found peace in you violence,
Now all I can hear is silence, I'm in need of a savior,
Don't try and act like you're doing me a favor,
Just look at you're behavior, Another nightmare, I'm not a puppet,
You can't just string me along, I didn’t do anything wrong, I write a poem to express my feelings,
Suppose that's apart of my healing, I don't think this one needs a title.

Unwritten

Why should I have to keep this stuff hidden, My life should have been forbidden,

I need to let this out, I want to scream and shout,

I'm taking back all the things you took,

All the things I over look, I take a deep breath,

This is a mistaken path,

I'm stronger and not going to be taken advantage of any longer,

I won't be weak, I will let this out, I will speak,

I'm slowly getting better, I'm just a lil child roaming all alone,

Look how much I've grown, I did it all on my own,

There's so many things I wished I'd have known,

I have lots of things left to learn, Now it's my turn,

I'm going to fly high, I have nothing left to deny,

Fly high in the sky, I just wish I could've asked why,

All my life I've been endangered, In my life I'm making a few changes,

I'll make a difference and shine my light,

For myself I will always fight,

So many words left unspoken, All the times I was left alone and broken,
I always have my finger on self destruct, All my life I've been stuck,
The rest remains unwritten.

Wedding day

Today should be the day we get married, Shit I'm worried,
Maybe I dodge a bullet, Maybe I should chase a fake escape,
I will wait a bit, What the fuck is this shit,
Fuck it I'll just get drunk, I'm craving the shit I had,
Your a maniac, I don't want to be in the way you act,
Why did you have to be so abusive and mean,
I got myself clean, maybe it was all just a dream,
My emotions will be the death of me,
I don't know who I'm meant to be, I'm smoking for medication,
My eyes are in radiation, Let me give you the real,
Writing just to feel, Pretty white dress,
Why did you leave me in this mess, Your giving me pretty words to impress,
How did it come to this? How did it escalate to this?
Why did you do this? Today should have been our

wedding day,

You left me with my heart scared and grey.

Well being

All I can do is fake a smile and fake it one day at a time,
I know I self halm I take a breath and keep calm,
I've got scars no one sees, Can you hold me till it closes,
I know I'm craving love or even to be above,
It's another day and I made it, I spend my life running,
I don't know what from, To my demons I succumb,
How can I be so fucking dumb, Shit! I feel so numb,
I don't know who I've become, I'm so frightened of myself,
Inside I'm dyeing, Trying to fake a smile, Like I'm happy,
But I'm not this world is taking everything I've got,
Would you walk in my shoes and tell me you give a damn,
Am I doing something wrong, Why can't I find a

place I belong,
I can't face this, People just take the piss,
I'm fine just by myself, Putting forward my health,
I'm so sick of this bullshit that keeps on coming,
it's so fucking numbing, People taking advantage of my kindness,
I'll never show you my weaknesses, Self esteem broken,
I'm always on the phone, I fight battles down here on my own,
I forgot about myself, I'm always putting myself at the bottom of the shelf,
I haven't been myself for months, I know I get distant that's when I need you to pull me closer,
I just need someone to tell me I'm not a loser,
I know I can't always say when I need holding, This life is revolting,
It's leaving me scolded, All I need is a helping hand,
How to show it remains a mystery, Hell fuck it the rest is history,
The right person has the strings to my heart,
This life always has me on alert, So I don't suffer any more hurt,

Sometimes my mind is blocked, Me and you are interlocked,

I felt as a kid I was a burden, Shit! Sorry am I being to blunt,

Would you prefer me to be less of a cunt,

All my life people have took pieces of me away,

I kept silent with nothing left to say,

Why did you have to turn around and leave,

C'mon Becky be brave, I know people don't want to be around me,

One day I'll find someone that's happy that they found me,

I'm always overwhelmed, I'm hiding in the shadows,

Drinking to numb the feels, Bits of me that everyone else steals,

I'm alone inside my head, Maybe I'd be better of dead,

Nah! fuck that! I'll stay here and fight instead.

Words

All the words they say echo in my head,

The voices fill me with dread, They make me wish I was dead,

You took away my choice and I lost my voice,

All that's left is that deafening echo, A hurricane,

All I want is my love to be found, I got pinned to the ground,

Something aint quite right and it's weighing me down,

Fuck it! I'll strengthen my crown,

All the things you said and did, I wish I could get rid,

All these secrets I kept hid,

I only stayed because that's all I thought I was worth,

So I tumble to the ground with a deafening thud,

So when is everything going to be said and done,

Fuck you expectation, This is so suffocating,

All the love I gave was never enough,

This is getting so tough, I'm crying with desperation,

I'm so tired of my pretending, I'm sure I've reached the end,

All I ever wanted was a friend, All the noise is a constant echo,

They all echo in my head, The voices fill me with dread,

I've been drowning within my mind, All I needed was a sign,

That these wounds will disappear and I won't live in constant fear,

I see them in every reflection, I'm seeing all my imperfections,

I hope it'll pass but damn! I hit the ground with a crash.

Write it

I need to write it now while it's in my head,
Are you pissed that I’m not in your bed?
Hang on! let me find my voice,
I'm living life like I have a choice,
I'm as cold as ice, In my life I live like I have a choice,
Write it, Don't fight it,
What's up do you want a slice?
This cake is amazing, I am changing,
My life I am paving,
This is in my words so let me speak,
I'm at the top of my spire,
I'm filled with fire,
I'm embracing my secret desire,
You don't need a preview,
This new me you won't know,
I was born to grow, I'm always in a bad mood,
You can't mess up my life, Alright
By now I’m used to your kind,
I need some distance, I'm making a difference,
I’ve been down this hole before,

Here is where I will lie,

I don't want to hear from you one more time,

You stabbed me in the back,

Another day, Another breakdown,

I'm stressed out, I'm not okay,

I'm begging on my knees,

This just goes on, on and on,

Sorry the person you are trying to reach is no longer fucking available.

Your mum

Your mum should have had an abortion,

Your not worth anything, Anything you say now doesn't mean a thing,

I don't know what happened to my plan, Of you I'm not a fan,

My attention is preoccupied, I've known all the classics of abuse,

Me you will no longer use, I'm made of snake skin,

This battle you won't win,

You won't control me, So do what you like I no longer care,

So do your worst, Give me your best shot, Your the one that's going to rot,

How strong I am you seemed to have forgot, When the day comes,

You'll think what have I done I won't be that person anymore,

I'll be successful so don't be so disrespectful,

You don't know me, I would rather suck dick than listen to you,

Don't even try to push my buttons to try to make

me react,

Your in the past, You will kick yourself for ever letting me go,

Yeah! your mum should have an abortion so she didn't have you,

for a son.

A Thank You

I would like to thank Anna for giving me this journal,

Also for sharing this journey with me, She enabled me to be me,

Also for being there to support me,

I would also like to give thanks to Sharon my best friend,

She's supported me threw every heartbreak, meltdown and mistakes,

Thank you for always being by my side,

I would also like to thank destiny whose my goddaughter,

she helped me and gave me the title of my book,

I would also like to give a huge thanks to Chris the back bone in my life,

He gives me strength without him this wouldn't have been possible,

Thank you for always being by my side and encouraging me,

You're not just Chris your the love of my life, my happiness and my soul mate,

I would also love to give a huge thanks to Jayne for always being there,
For always giving me advice,
So I would just like to say a huge Thank you to you all,
Without all of you I wouldn't be where I am today,
So thank you to you all,
Love from your little catastrophe.

Printed in Great Britain
by Amazon